EXPLANATION OF THE FAITH OF THE ARMENIAN CHURCH

Nerses IV the Gracious
Catholicos of Armenia

Translated by: D.P. Curtin

Dalcassian Publishing Company
PHILADELPHIA, PA

EXPLANATION OF THE FAITH OF THE ARMENIAN CHURCH

Copyright @ 2009 Dalcassian Publishing Company

All rights reserved. No part of this publication may be reproduced, distributed, or transmitted in any form or by any means, including photocopying, recording, or other electronic or mechanical methods, without the prior written permission of the publisher, except in the case of brief quotations embodied in critical reviews and certain other non-commercial uses permitted by copyright law. For permission request, write to Dalcassian Publishing Company at dalcassianpublishing at gmail.com

ISBN: 979-8-8690-8440-8 (Paperback)

Library of Congress Control Number:
Author: Curtin, D.P. (1985-)

Printed by Ingram Content Group, 1 Ingram Blvd, La Vergne, Tennessee

First printing edition 2009.

EXPLANATION OF THE FAITH OF THE ARMENIAN CHURCH

EXPLANATION OF THE FAITH OF THE ARMENIAN CHURCH

Made by order of the Emperor Manuel Komnenos in the year 1166 AD,
By the Patriarch Nerses IV Shnorhali (the Gracious), Catholicos of Armenia

Although the poverty of ideas and words does not allow us to undertake abstract discussions beyond our strength, and to sprinkle into the sea of your knowledge one more drop, nor to add to your celestial wisdom a weak ray of our intelligence, however the order of Your Imperial Majesty, which was transmitted to us by a servant of his court, inspired our humility with the boldness to present here in writing the explanation of the dogmas of our faith.

EXPLANATION OF THE FAITH OF THE ARMENIAN CHURCH

Moreover, divine law requires us to give what we have, whether much or little, to the one who asks. If we must give it to everyone, this precept must be observed with even more reason with regard to the greatest of us all. It is therefore with pleasure that we fulfill this duty imposed on us. It is not a new construction for which we are laying the foundations, but we are showing an edifice built with perfect materials, which fire cannot attack, placed *on the foundation of the apostles, prophets* and orthodox doctors. It is not an artificial eloquence that animates us, but the truth of the Holy Spirit, as it has been taught to us by those who have received his inspiring breath within them. We want to present our ideas, without trying to hide the darkness of heresy under the luminous appearance of the true faith, as those who themselves have this criminal habit imagine towards us; and we will record in writing what is contained in the secret of our soul, taking as witness the Holy Spirit who searches hearts, and who judges and examines everything.

Although we previously submitted to the appreciation of an eminently pious prince the explanation of our faith, which you yourself read, and although we considered it superfluous to repeat the same things, remembering the advice of him who said that *prolixity tires*; nevertheless, as this statement is required of us by your Majesty's order, we are ready to obey and add to what we have previously said, so that a second and third repetition will bring out the truth of our words. We will therefore begin with the point which first attracts our attention.

Dogmas.

Instructed by the holy Doctors of the Church, we confess that God the Father is distinct as a person, that he is without beginning and eternal, that God the Son was born of the eternal Father, not in the manner of creatures, but outside of time, and that the Holy Spirit emanates and proceeds from the Father by an ineffable mode.

The Father is called Father, because he is the cause of the birth of the Son, and of the procession of the Holy Spirit.

EXPLANATION OF THE FAITH OF THE ARMENIAN CHURCH

The Son is called Son, not because of a material birth, like ours, as the blind in spirit believe, but because he comes from the essence of the Father and is not not a creature, his birth being ineffable and beyond our understanding.

He is called the only Son, because no being, neither before him nor after him, proceeded in essence from the Father. It is also called Word, because its birth is immaterial, like the idea which springs from our mind.

It is not as in the mortal condition of man and by birth that the Father is before the Son; but as the Father is eternal, so the Son is eternal with the eternal Father, and is co-eternal with him from the beginning to the end, just as the rays coexist with the brightness of the sun, for this It is not the sun which appears before the light, but both appear at the same time. Likewise, the light of the Son comes from the light of the Father and is co-eternal with him. And as there is no brightness without light, nor an image without an original, so the Father never existed without the Son, nor the Son without the Father; the Son being the splendor of his glory and the reflection of his substance. The glory is God, and the splendor of his glory is the Son. The original is the Father, and the visible image of God the Father is the Son. This is why we recognize the Son as consubstantial with the Father, and cooperating with him in creation.

We confess that the Holy Spirit is the true Spirit of God, and we do not compare Him to created spirits, because He has the same name; just as we do not assimilate the only Son, in his essence, to those who are children of God by grace. The Holy Spirit differs from created spirits, in that he must be called the Spirit of God; proceeding, without beginning or end, from a Father who has neither beginning nor end, from all eternity, being perfect, incomprehensible and indescribable to creatures; emanating, as to its essence, from the Father alone, and, by his power and by the effusion of graces, equal to the Father and the Son, as we see by the words of the Son, when he says of the Holy Spirit: *He will not speak from himself, but he will take from mine and he will declare it to you, because everything that my Father has is mine* .

EXPLANATION OF THE FAITH OF THE ARMENIAN CHURCH

The Holy Spirit has no beginning in time, he does not experience changes of modality, conditions to which creatures are subject; but it conceals all the depths of the mysteries of God and reveals everything hidden in these mysteries; he is consubstantial with the Father and the Son, in his eternity, and participating in creation as being equal to them in power and glory.

We confess that these three persons are contained and united in one Godhead. We do not separate them from each other in their essence, as Arius taught; but we believe and we recognize in the Holy Trinity a single essence, a single sovereignty, a single power and a single glory. We likewise reject the opinion of Sabellius of Libya, a disciple of the Jews, who confused the three persons into one; but we distinguish these three persons as inseparable, and we unite them, distinguishing them one from the other, following the orthodox doctrine of the holy Fathers.

We therefore confess three persons, neither more nor less, and one single essence or nature without dividing it into three by the number of persons; and we conform to what the Church proclaims in the hymn of the seraphim, uniting the three glorified persons in one sovereignty and divinity. For If the Father is unbegotten, if the Son is begotten, and if the Holy Spirit is an emanation by way of procession, it does not follow from this that they differ from each other in their essence, like Adam, Seth and Eve; for the first, unbegotten, the second, born of a father, and Eve, although unbegotten, but nevertheless taken from Adam, really differ from each other by their very essence.

None of the three divine persons, equally adorable, outweighs the others in essence; and, although the Father is called great, he is only so described because of his primordiality and not because of his essence. For in his essence he is equal to the Son and the Holy Spirit; and the divinity of the Father was never incomplete, that is to say at first small, and then more and more perfect; as if there had existed a time when he would not have been God the Father as having no son, and when he would not have been wise as not containing wisdom in himself; and as if he had been weak, because he did not have power in him (for Jesus Christ, according to the words of the Apostle, *is the power and wisdom of*

God); as if it had been irrational, because the Word would not yet have been with him, which, according to the evangelist Saint John, was in the beginning with God; as if he had not been a quickener, because there would have been a time when he did not have the quickening spirit with him. But the Father is always the Father, having with him invariably the Word, power, wisdom and life; and the Son is always the eternal Son of the Father, forever with him; likewise, the Holy Spirit is always the Spirit of God, eternally with God.

The Father is the principle, and the Son and the Holy Spirit emanate from this principle, without limits of time and without cause. The Father pre-exists by himself, the Son and the Holy Spirit have their origin in the Father, but from all eternity and before all things, creators with the Father and of time and of all that is subject to time, of beings intellectuals and material beings, called by them from nothingness to life.

We confess that only one of the three persons, the Son, acting by the will of the Father and the Holy Spirit, and announced by the archangel Gabriel, descended on the earth created by him, but without leaving the places where he exercised his providential power, and remaining, without being diminished, in the living room from which he had descended. He who was incomprehensible to creatures wanted to enclose himself in the womb of the Virgin and received from her a perishable body subject to sin like ours: the soul, the spirit and the flesh which he mixed with his essence. impeccable and free from corruption, and with whom he was *one* in an indivisible way. He did not change the material nature of his body into an immaterial nature; but from a sinful body he made, when he wanted, an impeccable body; from corruption to incorruptibility; of what was mortal, immortality; preserving in this union the divine nature and the human nature, without confusing them. Conceived and enclosed for nine months in the womb of the Virgin, he was born from her without altering his immaculate virginity, receiving both from his Father an immaterial birth, and from his mother a birth following the flesh. Son of God, he became Son of man, without one being the Son of God and the other the Son of man; hypothesis by which an only son would have constituted two sons, as Nestorius taught in a blasphemous manner.

For the Word did not enter the body, but was incarnate, not by a change, but by a union affected in the womb of the Virgin. The Word was not materially formed into a body, by a creative operation, as some heterodox believe, but he received from the Virgin a body, not foreign to her, but part of her substance. It was not apparent that he passed through it, as through a canal, as Eutyches and his adherents falsely supposed; but he has truly clothed himself with a body of the substance of Adam, by a new and marvelous union, which is above all similarity. For, since the beginning of time, there has never been such a union of Creator and creature; it is only in a way and not with perfect accuracy that we can compare the union of soul and body with the union of divinity and humanity, as the saint says Gregory of Nyssa, in his Book on Nature, in the discourse on the union of soul and body, where he expresses himself thus: "Porphyry, this adversary of Jesus Christ (the objections of our enemies are strong against us and were not fought), gives similar testimony in his second speech. Here are his words: *A substance cannot be said to be filled by a substance which is other, while retaining its grandeur whole and unaltered; but through the rapprochement it converts it into its own nature* . Porphyry says this of the union of soul and body. If these words are true of the soul, in relation to its immortality, how much more must they be just in relation to the Word of God, which is truly and exactly immaterial!

We also believe that the Word, who, according to the words of Saint John, *became flesh,* did not become incarnate by losing his divine essence, but that he truly united himself with the body, and became made flesh, while remaining immaterial, as he was from the beginning. It is not because one was flesh and the other spirit; but it is the same and only Jesus Christ who is flesh and spirit; flesh by the humanity he took on, and spirit by the divinity he possessed; the same, visible and invisible, tangible and intangible, perishable and imperishable, temporal and eternal. Son of man and Son of God, consubstantial with the Father by his divinity and consubstantial with us by his humanity. Not being, because of this, a double person, but remaining the same being and the same person, formed of two natures united in Jesus Christ by an indivisible union, but without confusion. Although the human mind is too weak to fathom this mystery, which is above all intelligence, yet nothing is impossible for the divine power. For if the soul and the body are the creation of God, and if these two contrary entities can form a nature such that neither loses its essence by uniting,

EXPLANATION OF THE FAITH OF THE ARMENIAN CHURCH

how much more is it possible to the all-powerful divine nature to become flesh and remain immaterial, to unite with our human nature, which was created, and to preserve intact the uncreated nature that the Word receives from the Father!

Just as we confess that from two natures or substances one person was formed, and that in this union one of these two natures was not absorbed by the other; in the same way we admit, with regard to the two wills, that the divine will in Jesus Christ was not contrary to the human will, or the latter contrary to the divine will; but that in a single being there was a double will, according to the difference of times; that it was sometimes divine, when Christ wanted to manifest his all-powerful divinity, and sometimes human, when he wanted to show himself in the humble condition of humanity. This double will be not an indication of antagonism, but of their mutual independence; for the human will did not combat the divine will, as happens in us, *where the flesh has desires contrary to those of the spirit,* but the human will be subordinate to the divine will. Indeed, when the Lord wanted and allowed it, the body experienced what was proper to it, as was seen during the prayer which preceded the Passion, and during the temptation after the forty days fast, when it allowed human nature to feel hunger. And although he indicated a difference between the will of the Father and his own, saying: *Not as I will, but as you will,* this expression is a sign of assent, like that of a son towards his father, and not in opposition. This explanation is confirmed by another passage, where he maintains the will proper to the divinity, and where he distances the will of the flesh: *I came down from heaven, not to do my will, but that of my father.* The words *that came down from heaven* prove that his divinity was immaterial, and not his body, which he only took on when he came to earth. But, moreover, who will dare to separate in the divinity the will of the Son from that of the Father? If the Son, to show what is the will of the Father, says to us: *This is the will of my Father, that those who have faith in me have eternal life*, and if, therefore, the will of the Father is to give eternal life to those who believe in the Son, is this not at the same time the will of the Son? This alone is sufficient to prove agreement and exclude any idea of opposition. Saint Gregory the Theologian is explicit on this point: "According to the words of the Son to the Father, he says: *"Not my will be done, but yours, which is also mine*, Christ wanted to make it known that his will is the same as that of the Father; for if all that is of the Father is also of the

EXPLANATION OF THE FAITH OF THE ARMENIAN CHURCH

Son, it is evident that the will of the Father is that of the Son, and the will of the Son that of the Father."

As we have said, there was, through the unique and absolute power of the divinity, a double will, divine and human, without opposition. We believe that the actions performed in this union were equally divine and human. We do not attribute to the immaterial divinity of Christ alone his most sublime actions, and to his humanity separated from his divinity the actions of an inferior order; indeed, if it had been so, how could one say that the Son of man came down from heaven, or that he is a crucified God, and that his blood is divine? But we confess that the divine actions and the human actions of Christ were those of the same person, who sometimes, like God, performed divine actions, and sometimes, as man, human actions. This is what the economy of his whole life proves, from the beginning to the end.

Although he was conceived as a man, yet he was conceived by the Holy Spirit as God.

He was born of a woman as a man, but, like God, he preserved his mother's virginity after childbirth.

On the eighth day he was circumcised as a man, and he abolished bodily circumcision, teaching circumcision of the heart, as a lawgiver of circumcision.

He was presented after forty days in the temple, as a man, and he was recognized by Simeon, as God, deliverer of those who are held in bonds.

He fled before Herod, as a man, and he rejected idolatry from Egypt, as God.

He was baptized by Saint John, as a man; but, as God, he blotted out the sins of Adam by his baptism, and he was proclaimed as such, by the Father and the Holy Spirit.

New Adam, he was tempted like the old Adam; but, as the creator of Adam, he overcame the tempter, and, as God, he gave to the children of Adam power to crush the power of the enemy.

As a man, he suffered hunger, and, like God, he satisfied the multitude with a few loaves.

As a man he felt thirst, and as God he called to himself those who were thirsty and gave them to drink from the spring of life.

As a man, he felt weariness while walking, and, like God, he was the refuge of the afflicted and of sinners weighed down under the burden of their faults, to whom he gave his yoke gentle and easy to bear.

As a man he slept in a boat, and as God he walked on the waves and commanded the winds and the sea.

As a man, he paid the tax, and, as God, he ordered a stater to be taken from the mouth of the fish.

As a man, he prayed with us and for us, and, like God, he welcomed with his Father the prayers of us all.

As a man, he shed tears on the grave of his friend, and, like God, he dried up the tears of the sisters who mourned a brother, by resurrecting him.

As a man, he asked where Lazarus was buried, and, like God, he restored him to life four days after his death, calling to him aloud.

As a man he was betrayed for a pitiful sum of money, and as God he redeemed the world by the shedding of his precious blood.

EXPLANATION OF THE FAITH OF THE ARMENIAN CHURCH

He was dumb *as a lamb before his shearer,* according to human nature; but, by his divine nature, he is the Word of God, existing from the beginning, by whom *the heavens were established.*

As a man, he was attached to a cross between two thieves, and, like God, he veiled the stars with darkness and brought the good thief into paradise.

As a man, he drank the vinegar and tasted the gall that was presented to him, and, like God, he transformed the water into wine, and changed the bitterness into sweetness.

As a man he died; like God, he resurrected the dead by his omnipotence.

As man, he drank the chalice of death by his will, and, as God, he conquered death by his death.

He who died is no other than he who triumphed over death, but he is the same and the only one who is both dead and alive, and gives life; the one and same Jesus Christ, both man, of a mortal nature, and God, of an immortal nature; not divided into two hypostases by the division of the two natures, as if it were one which suffered and died, and the other which was impassible and immortal. But formed of two contrary natures, he experienced in his unity the effects of these two opposing natures: through human nature, the suffering and death imposed on humanity; by divine nature, impassibility and immortality. He who is dead in the body is the same who is alive in the divinity; the one who suffered, the same one who was impassive; he who, through fear, sweated blood, the same one who struck down those who rose up against him. He who was for a little while in humiliation and a little lower than the angels, and who was comforted by the angels, is the same who comforted all creatures. Creator of all beings with his Father, following divinity, he was a creature like us, following humanity.

EXPLANATION OF THE FAITH OF THE ARMENIAN CHURCH

The Apostles, sent by the Word, proclaimed him God and perfect man, by a union more perfect than that of soul and body.

His human soul, which he recommended to his Father, separated from his body; but the divinity remained indivisible in both at the same time; it remained with his rational soul, when he descended into hell, towards the souls who were held there, and it was inseparable from his body deposited in the tomb, not in part, but entirely in both.

It is the same who was both in the bosom of the Father and in the womb of the Virgin, on the throne of glory and in the manger of Bethlehem, at the right hand of the Father and on the cross, above the cherubim and in the grave, *for heaven and earth are filled with his glory* . He rose again on the third day, he who is our resurrection and our life, and ascended to the heavens which he had never left. He will come down one day to resurrect the race of Adam, and to judge in his righteousness the living and the dead according to their words, their thoughts, their actions and their faith, rewarding the good and condemning the wicked to torture.

It is the same who will reign with those who will be crowned with him throughout the centuries, discovering to all, and without veil, this science of faith which we possess today only imperfectly, of faith in the Father, to the Son and the Holy Spirit, to whom belong the glory and the power for all ages. Amen.

This exposition of our doctrine on the consubstantial Trinity, the one Divinity, and on the incarnation of the Son, an exposition which is in conformity with our profession of faith, and which we have made by order of Your Majesty, may it suffice for you for the moment , by providing the opportunity for Your Wisdom to make, following the words of the wise, new progress in wisdom.

EXPLANATION OF THE FAITH OF THE ARMENIAN CHURCH

Traditions of the Church.

Let us now say a few words about the traditions transmitted to us by the ancient Fathers, and against the opinions of those who do not admit them. We will make known the reasons which lead us to observe these traditions, and we will explain ourselves, God serving as our witness, in all sincerity and without ulterior motives.

Let us first speak of the bread of the holy Sacrifice, which we and the Romans use unleavened, and the other Churches fermented. Everyone, on both sides, tries to justify the custom to which they are attached. But he who loves the truth must not make himself the slave of customs like an ignoramus, or justify himself with vain words, used as a simple argument for discussion; on the contrary, he must travel in spirit through the spiritual paradise (I mean the holy books), and seek there the fruit of truth, and then taste it. Thus, with regard to the institution of the sacrament which we have just named, we find in these books the truth which we seek. The whole mystery of the incarnation of Jesus Christ, as well as the perfection of his flesh and blood, are announced by the prophets under various figures and in different words. And first at the table of Abraham, who was the type of the table of the upper room, the Lord ate, not the fermented bread, but the unleavened bread, as results from these words of Abraham to Sarah: "Hurry- you knead three measures of pure flour and make loaves of it baked in ashes." This same bread, a simple figure, when the Word had not yet become incarnate, he also used when he had become flesh, and, calling it his body, he divided it among the sons of Abraham, according to faith, instead of the veal and the unleavened grass that he had eaten in the shade of the Mambré oak. That the bread baked by Sarah was unleavened is evident from that which Lot gave to the angels; for it is written: "He baked unleavened bread and served it to them."

When the children of Israel were about to leave Egypt, Moses ordered them not to take fermented bread with them, to abstain entirely from it in their houses for seven days, and to eat for all that time. week, matzo bread only. This was the type of use of unleavened bread in the Holy Supper, and the seven days represent the seven ages of the world. By this commandment, the Lord willed that all those who depart from Egyptian unbelief, to make their way towards the land of promise, should not take with them the leaven of sin, but should nourish themselves with bread incorruptible and divine, both mystical and material, that is to say of the body of God, and *of the word which comes from his mouth*. Likewise, manna, which, according to the apostle Saint Paul, was the type of the bread of life, was eaten by the Jews in the desert, as unleavened bread.

And when God commanded Moses not to appear before him empty-handed, he wanted the showbread to be placed on the altar of propitiation every day, as an emblem of the body of Jesus Christ. That this bread was unleavened and not fermented is demonstrated by what the priest Abiathar said to David: "It is not impure bread (that is to say fermented) that is in my hands. , but sacred shewbread," which was unleavened. There are many such examples in ancient times; but let's come to those of the new law and the real ones.

When the true Lamb had tasted the mystical lamb and unleavened bread with lettuces, and fulfilled the precept of the old covenant, he instituted the new, according to the gospel account. Taking some bread from the table (it is obvious that it was unleavened bread, since it was the first day of the unleavened festival), he said: *This is my body.*

It is therefore appropriate that the body of him who was born of the Virgin, and who was immaculate, is represented by unleavened bread and not by fermented bread.

For us, who celebrate the holy Mystery with unleavened bread, we have these reasons and others provided by Holy Scripture to justify our use. Those who perform this sacrament with fermented bread can also rely on certain passages of Scripture to defend their rite. They first cite the Savior's praise of leaven, who compares it to the kingdom of heaven. It is true that it is not the sacrament of the sacred bread that is in question in this example, but the preaching of the Gospel, which entered the world as leaven enters flour, and which made ferment all those who believed in it, exciting them to the love of God.

EXPLANATION OF THE FAITH OF THE ARMENIAN CHURCH

Elsewhere, leaven is taken as the symbol of evil, in the sacred books, witness these words of Saint Paul: *Jesus Christ, our Passover, has been immolated. Therefore let us celebrate this festival, not with the old leaven, nor with the leaven of wickedness and malice, but with the unleavened bread of sincerity and truth* . And Gregory the Theologian, in his sermon on Passover, says that fermented bread cannot be the bread of life.

Although we have noted that this sacrament, which was transmitted to us by the Lord, had been accomplished with unleavened bread. However, the apostolic traditions cannot completely enlighten us on this point and teach us whether it is unleavened bread. or the fermented bread which was used in the first centuries of the Church. We only know that the faithful were commanded to bring the bread with which the holy mysteries were celebrated. Therefore, if the Holy Spirit had judged that one was pleasing to God, and not the other, he would have taught it to the Church, either through its Apostles, or through the mouth of the holy Doctors. But we know for sure that what pleases God is an orthodox faith and an irreproachable life. Provided that the sacrament is performed with right intentions and is pure of any heterodox opinion, the traditions or usages spoken of here, which are customs particular to each people, do not contain in themselves anything that could exceed or diminish the faith. Also, when the head, that is to say the faith, is firmly united to the supreme head, who is Jesus Christ, then the members, that is to say the traditions, are in good condition and come into being. help one another, for the glory of Christ our God.

The rest of our discussion now leads us to speak of the chalice of the blood of Jesus Christ. It is only among us, and not in other Churches, that by virtue of a tradition dating back to Saint Gregory, we use pure wine for the Eucharist, without mixing with water. The main reason for this usage comes from the fact that the blood of Jesus Christ is incorruptible through its union with the incorruptible Word; and it is in this spirit that the chalice of his blood receives only pure wine among us. This is made evident by the general name given to the wine; if, in fact, wine without a mixture of water is called *pure wine*, it is indubitable that when this mixture is added, the wine ceases to be a *pure wine* and can no longer be called that.

Moreover, when the Lord took the chalice in his hands, he said: *This is my blood, the blood of the new covenant,* and he added: *From now on I will no longer drink of this fruit of the vine until that day on which I will drink it again with you, in my Father's kingdom.* Blessed John Chrysostom, in explaining these words in his commentary on the Gospel of Saint Matthew, says: "He uproots another bad heresy down to the root. There are some who, in the holy mysteries, use water; but the Lord said: *Of this fruit of the vine,* and the vine bringeth forth wine, and not water." Those who mix water with wine try to divert the words of this holy doctor, by affirming that there were people who used only pure water to accomplish the holy Mystery, and that this is They are what Saint John Chrysostom speaks of, and not of those who mix water with wine. As for us, we have never heard of this kind of people, and we have not read anything anywhere about such a senseless heresy. Those who accomplish the mystery with wine mixed with water are perhaps right in doing so; but those who use pure water, in whose name do they perform it? Is it in the name of Jesus Christ? No, certainly, for the Savior, according to the Evangelists, took the wine in his hand and not the water, when he said: *This is my blood.* And as no one, except Jesus Christ, had instituted this sacrament, neither with wine nor with water, I conclude that everything that is said must be regarded as pure inventions and not as truth.

Those who mix water with wine base this traditional usage on the circumstance that two jets flowed from the side of Jesus Christ, one of blood and the other of water. But can we rightly think that this great and admirable miracle took place for the purpose of this sacrament? If God had had this in mind, it would have been enough for him to inspire some of the men animated by the Holy Spirit, the Apostles or the most illustrious doctors of the Church, with the thought of prescribing the pouring of water in the chalice of the Lord, and no one then would have opposed it. But it was not for this mixture to be effected that the water flowed with the blood from the side of the Savior, but rather to indicate the mystery of baptism into the death of Jesus Christ, according to the words of the apostle Saint Paul to the Romans: *Do you not know that all those who were baptized into Jesus Christ were baptized into his death?* Saint John Chrysostom, in his commentary on the Gospel of Saint John, says: "The Church was founded from the two jets which flowed from the side of Jesus Christ, for we are born for the second time by the water of baptism, and his blood nourishes us." Likewise, Saint Gregory of Nyssa, in his discourse on the burial of the Lord, said, putting these words into the mouth of Joseph of Arimathea: "I will touch his immaculate side, from which flowed, like from a fountain, the mysterious blood and regenerative water." Saint Ephrem of Syria also says: "A jet of water flowed from his body, to extinguish the fire of the first Adam and to erase the traces of the servitude which bowed him under the yoke of evil. Blood also flows from it as an effect of his mercy, for it is by this blood that he redeemed us from our servitude. And as all vitality is in the blood, it is through his blood that he revived our life." Several other doctors, alluding to this text of the Gospel, comment on it in the same way by relating water to the sacrament of baptism and blood to the sacrament of the Eucharist.

As we have already said, speaking of sacred bread, that the Lord requires of us, above all, true faith and blameless actions, and not the fulfillment of the holy mysteries with fermented bread rather than matzo; we will repeat the same thing when speaking of wine: whether we use it with water or without water, neither of these uses can earn us the praises of God or bring on our heads punishments. Only those will be glorified by him who offer their gifts to him with a holy heart and an upright spirit. But those who are defiled with impure thoughts and criminal actions, whether they celebrate with pure wine or with a mixture of water, must certainly expect to be punished.

If one of these two practices or the other had been in the formal will of God or his saints, they would have recorded it in writing, as was the case with the other precepts. Saint Paul, in his Epistle to the Corinthians, when speaking of the Eucharist, did not say in what way it should be celebrated, whether with fermented bread or unleavened bread, with a mixture of water or without water, but he mainly insisted on what God requires of us. *Let each one test himself,* he said, *and so eat of this bread and drink of this chalice; for whoever eats and drinks of it unworthily eats and drinks his own condemnation, not making due discernment of the body of the Lord.* Other interpreters of the divine oracles similarly recommend, not the distinction of matter, but a worthy preparation for the sacrament.

EXPLANATION OF THE FAITH OF THE ARMENIAN CHURCH

There still exists in the Armenian Church a tradition which dates from the most ancient times, according to which the feast of Christmas is celebrated on the same day as that of Epiphany. The reason for this custom is not accidental, but entirely mystical. In the first centuries, it was general in all the Churches, as is known to Your Wisdom; and although in the course of time, some Churches have made this single feast two separate feasts, we have preserved unaltered the tradition of Saint Gregory, based on the testimony of Saint Luke. This Evangelist, after having related how Zechariah became mute, adds: "It came to pass, when the days of his ministry were ended, that he returned to his house; and Elizabeth, his wife, became pregnant."

The time of Zechariah's priestly service consists, according to Saint Luke, of the five days of the Feast of the Atonement and the seven days of the Feast of Tabernacles, in all twelve days. The appearance of the angel and the silence of Zechariah occurred on the first day of the Feast of Atonement, that is to say the tenth day of the seventh month of the Hebrews (Tishri), September 27 of the Roman calendar. It is on this date that you others report the conception of Elizabeth, supposing that it was the same day on which this conception was announced by the archangel Gabriel that Zechariah returned to his house and that his wife Elizabeth became pregnant , while Zechariah had to wait until the end of the feast, as is proved by the account of the Evangelist, where it is said: *When the days of his ministry were ended, he returned to his house* . This house was located in the mountainous parts of Judea, far from Jerusalem. You thus place the Annunciation of the Virgin on March 25, and the Nativity of Jesus Christ on December 25, twelve days before us.

But we, who base ourselves on the words of Saint Luke, say that the conception of Elizabeth took place after the twelve days of the two feasts, which are called the days of the priesthood of Zechariah, had ended, that is to say -say the 23rd of the Hebrew month Tishri, or October 10.

According to this calculation, the Annunciation of the Virgin Mary must always fall on April 7 and Christmas on January 6. Thirty years later, on the same day of the month in which the Savior was born, although on a different day of the week, He was baptized in the Jordan, which is a perfectly accurate account. If he was, in fact, thirty years old, neither more nor less, it follows that the day of his baptism must have coincided with the day of his birth, counting thirty full years without adding anything. But if the nativity is earlier and precedes the baptism by twelve days, then there was no reason to say that *Jesus was about thirty years old,* but that he had entered his thirty-first year, as results from the naming of days. Indeed, at sunrise, we give the day a new name and not that of the day that has passed; it is the same for months and for years, where the first day is called by the name of the day begun and not of that which has passed. It is according to these carefully examined considerations that the holy Fathers of the first centuries decreed to celebrate, on the same day, the mystery of the nativity and baptism of Jesus Christ. We, by conforming to this rule, are only following their traditions.

There is, furthermore, another mystery to consider here. As the Savior was born, according to the flesh, of the Virgin, so he took a new birth by baptism, in the Jordan, in order to be an example for us. And as these are two births, although they differ in mystery and time, nevertheless we decided to celebrate both, on the same day, this first and this second nativity.

There are many other reasons which can justify the Armenian tradition, prove its agreement with the traditions of the first Fathers of the Church, and at the same time show that it is not arbitrarily that we remain apart from other peoples. , for the celebration of these solemnities. It is they, on the contrary, who, having first followed the same customs as us, changed them at will and now observe them in a new way.

Our Church has maintained this ancient custom in an invariable manner. Is it because of the distance from our country, or as a result of a split which gave rise to feelings of hatred? This is what we do not know. Hatred, in fact, not only opposes the introduction of new traditions, but it even strives to distance from ancient customs those who hate each other as adversaries; while ardent charity excites us to do not only what is convenient and easy, but what is painful and inopportune, out of condescension to those we love. Besides, as it seems to me, the main thing in this is not the date of the month or the name of the day, but only the aversion that results from it. For whatever day we celebrate a festival, if we do it without dispute, we please God.

What is greater than the solemnity of Easter, about which several Churches disagreed, as Eusebius of Caesarea relates? The inhabitants of Asia Minor celebrated it on Thursday, as in the ancient Law, according to the teaching of the Evangelist Saint John, while the Church of Rome celebrates it on Sunday, the day of the Resurrection of Our Lady. -Lord. But, after some light discussions, agreement was reestablished on both sides by Saint Irenaeus, disciple of the Apostles. He said to one and the other: "The truth of the faith being the same for all, it is not appropriate to argue over a difference in the time of festivals; for whatever is done for the glory of God is accepted by him also. This is how the coloring of the skin, whether it is brown or white, cannot do harm to the body, if the constitution of the body is healthy. It is the same for those who have true faith: variety in the observance of festivals or in any point of ecclesiastical discipline cannot in any way prejudice their salvation.

Thus, the trisagion, by which the three Persons of the Trinity are invoked in your churches, and which we address only to the Son, is a mystical and sublime hymn in both cases, if it is not the subject of controversy; that if, on the contrary, it gives rise to disputes, it is no longer a song of praise, but of blasphemy.

Some of you, slandering us, object that, in the trisagion, we say the *Trinity crucified;* but ours, in their turn, answer you that you do not call him who was crucified for us *God strong and immortal in death,* but that you call him simply *Man;* and both parties are trying to win a regrettable victory in this debate. Although we address this canticle to the Son alone, according to the tradition of the first Fathers of the Church, there are nevertheless certain offices where we sing the hymn of the seraphim in honor of the Trinity. If both parties could agree by the will of God, then everything could be arranged by the addition of a few words. A first time, the trisagion, conceived in these terms: *God strong and immortal*, would be consecrated to the Father; the second time to the Son, and the third time to the Holy Spirit; so that each of the three Persons was glorified in an equal and complete manner, and not half and in part, as would be the case

EXPLANATION OF THE FAITH OF THE ARMENIAN CHURCH

if we said the Father *God* only, without adding *strong and immortal;* and the Son, *strong*, omitting the words *God and immortal;* and the Holy Spirit, *immortal*, neglecting the words *God* and *strong*. On the contrary, it is necessary to apply these three attributes to the three Persons and to each of them separately.

It is from the same source that raises an unfounded objection concerning the holy cross, namely whether or not the wood from which it was made should be joined by means of nails. In this regard, there are no positive precepts among us. And, moreover, according to what teaching could we admit that the cross must be honored in one aspect and disdained in another? Is it by a command from God? But there is no such thing. These difficulties undoubtedly come from the pitfalls that Satan sets up for us, who wants the sign which serves to defeat him to be insulted by the very people who revere it, and who would like to see this sign destroyed by their hands, in order to make it a game for him, and for them a cause of perdition. If it were not this, what harm could a nail do to faith? It is obvious that this nail is only placed by us so that the arms of the cross remain superimposed, without being able to separate; and, moreover, what completes the proof of what I am putting forward is that since the gold or silver crosses are not made from two pieces, we do not put a nail in them. We cannot suppose that the true cross was without nails, because it could not have supported the weight of a body.

According to a symbolic idea, the tree of the cross, or the perpendicular part, is the emblem of the Divinity, the transverse part, that of humanity, and the nail which connects them together signifies the love which unites God to the men. What harm is there for the soul whether or not nails are used in this situation? A dispute on such a subject is childishness, unworthy of a man of mature age.

Concerning the ceremony of blessing the cross, which we adopted from the first Fathers of the Church, and on which your doctors raise difficulties, we will be short. We ourselves found it in this country, written in Greek characters in an Old Testament. Is it more appropriate to first read the divine words taken from the Prophets, the Apostles, the Evangelists, and to recite the prayers that the priest pronounces on a new cross, and then to erect it towards the East and from there [...] love [...] or should we simply prostrate ourselves before a material object, without having blessed it, as if every object of quadrangular shape, which is offered to the eye in paintings or everywhere else in any other way, was worthy of adoration?

Shall I still speak of the images of the Savior and the saints, against which some of our people, ignorant people, show aversion? You are scandalized by this, regarding this behavior as a prescription imposed by us on our entire nation. But we, as well as all those who follow our example, understand and teach that in the presence of the cross which bore a God, it is not to a material object that we pay homage, but to the invisible God who there was attached; likewise, in the image of the Savior, it is not a material painting that we adore, but Christ, who is the image of God the Father, invisible.

We honor and glorify the images of the saints, regarding them as our mediators and our protectors with God: that is to say, we offer our adorations to God by taking them as our intercessors; for it is only to the image of the Creator, and not to creatures, that adoration is due. The image and the name are the same thing, one being a simple form, and the other a simple significant designation, one reminding the eye and the other the ear the idea of a thing.

We also prostrate ourselves before men, not only before those who are worthy, but even before those who are unworthy, insofar as they carry within themselves, during their life, the image of the Divinity, it is that is, the soul. When it is separated from the body, then it only belongs to the bodies of the saints to be honored; for, as it is written, *God rests in their bones.* But the bodies of those who have not attained holiness should not be the object of such homage, because they contain nothing divine in them. The name and the image alone, regardless of the substance, even if they belong to saints, just as to people devoid of holiness, must not be honored. For the Creator alone is to be present in all places by his essence; therefore, his invisible essence is worshiped in his visible image and in his name. The essence of created beings is contained only in the place where it is found and not in all places. Since the visible image of a creature does not contain in itself its invisible type, as is the case with the image of the Creator, it follows that one should not worship the image of a human creature on its own. equal to the image of God. On this point there is a testimony from the Apostle who says that, as a result of this full submission of the Son, clothed with our nature, towards his Father, a submission which went as far as the death of the cross, the Father gave him to reward *a name that is above every name.* How this name is above every name is what the Apostle explains in the same passage: *So that at the name of Jesus,* says he, *every knee should bow, in heaven and on earth and in hell.*

If then the name of Jesus Christ is, like his image, above every name and the object of worship of all that is in heaven and on earth, according to the words of the Apostle, by therefore his name must be glorified equal to his image, as we have said. Thus, it is not appropriate to consider as signs of adoration the image and name of beings of a servile nature, equal to the name and image of the Lord. We other creatures must worship only the image, reproduced by painting, of our Creator and Savior.

As for the images of the faithful servants of God, who by their nature have been servants like us, we must honor and respect these images, according to the merit of those they represent. Their contemplation should excite us to imitate the virtuous life of those whose traits they remind us of and to take it as a model, while reflecting on the real afflictions they experienced. Let him who despises them not imagine that his disdain falls on a simple material image, but on the one it represents, whether it be that of the Lord himself or of his servants.

I will add a few words about the fast called *aradchavork* (that is to say, *preliminary),* and about which your party invented a fable.

A monk named Sergius, they claim, had a donkey and a dog; this dog always preceded his master to the places he went, and thereby announced his arrival, so that the populations would rush to meet him. It is because this dog always preceded its master, they add, that we gave the fast the name of the animal, according to the order of this same Serge. Such slander is worse than all the false doctrines of the pagans.

EXPLANATION OF THE FAITH OF THE ARMENIAN CHURCH

This is the fruit of hatred; when we hate someone, we block our ears so as not to hear good things said about them, and this good thing we consider to be a lie, while we eagerly welcome falsehoods and fables, and we welcome them. take for truths, as we see from this example alone. If we found ourselves in the darkness of ignorance, like that of idolatry, it would be impossible to impute to us such a ridiculous invention; but this cannot be done, now less than ever, when the whole earth is filled with the knowledge of God, and the torch of wisdom enlightens the world. The first reason why we call this fast *aradchavork* is because it precedes the Great Lent and is like its precursor. Secondly, it is because it is the first Lent that Saint Gregory imposed on the Armenian nation, when he was removed from the pit into which he had been thrown.

He then wanted those who had been struck with a celestial punishment to fast for five days, in order to make themselves worthy by this penance of obtaining their healing; this is why a large number of people now fast for these five days, according to ancient custom. Subsequently, it was considered appropriate to add this fast to that of the Ninevites, which the Syrians and Egyptians observe rigorously. In our country, the reason why we celebrate, at the end of this first Lent, the memory of Saint Sergius, general of the army, is because, during the year, January 30 is the day when Saint Sergius shed his blood for the faith of Jesus Christ.

This is why we decided to celebrate his feast on Saturday of the same week, just as on the first Saturday of Great Lent all Christians celebrate the memory of Saint Theodore.

This Serge, according to his history, was a general, originally from Cappadocia, at the time of Constantine the Great. He distinguished himself by his valor in the wars against the Barbarians, and by his ardent faith in Jesus Christ. When Julian the Apostate ascended the throne, the pious Sergius took refuge in Persia, and it was there that with his son he bore witness to Jesus Christ before King Sapor, and having had his head cut off, he received the palm of martyrdom.

EXPLANATION OF THE FAITH OF THE ARMENIAN CHURCH

This is all I have to say about the traditions relating to our faith and the discipline of our Church. When this statement is read before Your august Majesty, may not your high wisdom think that our words have been dictated by a spirit of falsehood or adulation, as if we had retraced lines which are not already engraved in our hearts. Whoever does this deserves that *God scatter his bones,* according to the word of the prophet concerning the hypocrites. For the torch of faith must not be hidden under a bushel in the darkness; but it must be placed on the candlestick of truth. Hidden faith is ungodliness, because then there is fraud and not truth.

May the Lord deign to fertilize the seed of our words, spread on the fertile soil of your ideas, and make it multiply. This seed will not be choked by thorns or deprived of roots and dried up or eaten by the birds of the air. May we reap the fruits of peace and love for the great work that you are pursuing, not in the same measure or double the gain that has been entrusted to the earth, but in a hundredfold of a triple measure. Thus, you and those who cultivated this spiritual field will be rewarded according to the quantity of the harvest, by Our Lord Jesus Christ, to whom belong the glory and honor, as well as to the Father and the Holy Spirit, now, and forever, for ever and ever. Amen.

The Scriptorium Project is the work of a small group of lay people of various apostolic churches who are interested in the preservation, transmission, and translation of the works of the early and medieval church. Our efforts are to make the works of the church fathers accessible to anyone who might have an interest in Christian antiquities and the theological, philosophical, and moral writings that have become the bedrock of Western Civilization.

To-date, our releases have pulled from the Greek, Syriac, Georgian, Latin, Celtic, Ethiopian, and Coptic traditions of Christianity, and have been pulled from sundry local traditions and languages.

Other Selections from the Armenian Church Series:

Explanation of the Faith of the Armenian Church by Nerses IV the Gracious, Catholicos of Armenia (July 2009)

The Life of Mashtots by Koriun the Iberian (Nov. 2012)

Letter to Kiwron, Catholicos of Iberia by Movses II, Catholic of Armenia (Nov. 2013)

Canons of the Synod of Partav by Sion I, Catholicos of Armenia (Dec. 2013)

The History of the Holy Cross of Aparank by St. Gregory of Narek (Feb. 2014)

Armenian Synaxarium: Volume I- Month of Navasard (Oct. 2018)

The Geography by Ananias of Shirak (Dec. 2020)

www.ingramcontent.com/pod-product-compliance
Lightning Source LLC
LaVergne TN
LVHW061044070526
838201LV00073B/5165